Don't Let Fear Stop You

Micaiah J. Crenshaw

Presented To:

____

From:

____

Date

____

DEDICATION

I would like to dedicate this book to my mom and my family.

CONTENTS

ENCOURAGE

I WOULD LIKE TO ENCOURAGE ALL THE KIDS IN THE WORLD. I WANT
YOU TO KNOW THAT I WROTE THIS BOOK ESPECIALLY FOR YOU WHO ARE
FEARFUL. DON'T BE AFRAID, AND NEVER LET FEAR
STOP YOU!

THE GAME PLAN

She Kicks! She scores! Hey! I'm Micaiah and I'm really good at some sports, like soccer. I don't play on a real team yet, because sometimes I have a fear of meeting new people and not winning a real game so I just play soccer with my friends, at school during gym, and recess.

One day I was out playing a game of soccer with my friends and as we took a little break, I imagined that my mom and I were at my soccer game. Hey, you know what will really be cool? If you would Imagine with me that you are there too, (music in my head) bum bum da da do.

Ok, back to where we started. My mom raced down the field as I played. Go! Go! She screamed as she cheered me on. I was running and running as fast as I could, then all of a sudden fear came over me because I knew my team mates were counting on me to score the winning goal; so I called time out. Everybody stopped and starred: my coach, my team mates, and all the fans. All eyes were on me. My mom yelled out from the side lines and asked, "are you alright Micaiah," I yelled back and said "yes Ma'am."

Instantly, I walk off the field and laid down on the bench thinking about what I could do to score the final goal so that I wouldn't disappoint my teammates and help us win. Then all of a sudden I got it! I jumped up, got back in the game, and out of no-where I ran and I kicked the ball so hard that I landed on my bum basket, and the ball landed in the net, making it thc winning scorc!

The crowd went wild! I could hear the announcer...The winnnnnner is Micaiah Crenshaw! and her team! The crowd cheers again and my mom was screaming! Then the interviewer comes up to me and asked " How do you feel about this Micaiah?" I feel great! I'm so excited! about being the best soccer player and winner of all times. Thank you all. Thank you America for this great opportunity guys! You all are so amazing!

While I was so in the moment all of a sudden I heard my friends voices yelling! Micaiah! Micaiah! What are you doing! I thought Heeey! Micaiah Keep using your imagination this is really good! As I raised up off the bench I could hear one of them say ugh! there she goes dreaming again! I yelled back, I'm coming! I'll be right there. As I walk back over to play, I thought to myself, Wow! That was soooo real! Well, back to reality. Honestly, the reality of all this is that my mom was proudly watching me and a group of my friends play a game of soccer in our back yard.

Meanwhile, as we continued to play our neighborhood game of soccer I started running up and down our backyard waiting for a chance to score, and then came the final play. The ball landed right in front of me, boy was I scared, but I thought this is it, no turning back now. As soon as I was ready to kick the ball, I glanced over and all I could see was that my mom had her eyes closed with both hands covering her mouth, as if she was nervous or maybe even scared. I'm not sure.

Then instantly, boom! it happened! I made it! The ball went shooting like a rocket right into the net and I landed on my bum basket. Yes! I scored the winning goal point! just like I imagined! Suddenly, my mom ran over and hugged me very tight while all my friends yelled out Gooo!! Micaiah, Micaiah, Micaiah you made it! OMG! This was Awesome! dreams really do come true! I'm so glad I didn't give up and let fear stop me!

I ASKED MY MOM

I asked my mom what does fear mean and she told me to look it up in the dictionary. So, I looked up the word fear and I found out that fear is:

A. To be afraid or scared of

B. To be frightened of

C. To be uneasy about

D. To feel anxious

E. An emotion experienced by some specific pain or danger

Now that I know what fear means, I finally understand some of the stuff that I was feeling on the inside of me. This also help me to realize that because I didn't know what was going on with me, I was also afraid and ashamed to express it out loud to anyone for fear of what they might think of me.

HAVE COURAGE

One day I said to my mom, "how can God help me with fear?" And she told me to pray an ask God to give me the courage to overcome my fears every time I become afraid of something. Then, I said, "how will He help me" and she said, "go in a room by myself and pray and listen for His voice and you will hear Him speak and He will tell you."

I did what she said and I heard His voice say to me "don't let fear stop you." I was so happy that I heard His voice it really gave me courage. It was amazing to me! I ran as fast as I could to tell my mom what God said to me! She said, "really Micaiah, He really said that?" She said, "don't you lie to me" and I said, "mom I'm not lying" I'm telling you the truth God really did say those words to me.

My mom hugged me and said always remember what God spoke to you and always listen for His voice. Then she told me to read the scripture that she always says to me, my brothers and sister: One thing is for sure, I will always remember that day.

2 Timothy 1:7, for God have not given us the spirit of fear; but of power, and of love, and of a sound mind.

I FACED MY FEARS

Now that I have courage and a better idea and understanding of what fear really is, let's take a look at a list of my fears that I overcame. Who knows, maybe you are like me; if you are then, look at how I overcame my fears, and maybe this will help you overcome yours.

1. **<u>Swimming</u>** - with lots of practice along with the help and encouragement from my sister. I'm no longer afraid, and now I can swim without assistance.

2. **<u>Riding a bike</u>** - this was really, really hard and scary for me but my biggest fear was, I didn't want to fall and hurt myself. However, I had lots and lots of falls but because I wanted to learn so bad I kept on trying, and I kept on practicing. And Guess what? I finally learned to ride my bike and now I truly believe I'm the best bike rider ever.

3. **<u>Skating</u>** - this was hard and a real challenge for me because I didn't want to fall in front everyone, but I did! OMG! I was so embarrassed! I didn't want to hurt myself, and I did! But I was very determined; every time we would go skating I would hold on to the rails at the skating rink and practice and fall until one day I finally got it! skating sure feels awesome!

4. **<u>Sleeping alone</u>** - every time that I would sleep by myself, I always felt like something was going to get me- like a monster or something. It wasn't easy overcoming this fear. After many nights of crying, sleeping in my parent's room, my sister room, with night lights on, and everyone sending back to my room when I would fall asleep; things didn't get any better for me. My mom would always say to me pray before you go to sleep that God and His angels would protect me and so would she. One night I did just that and I felt safe and I

finally realized that nothing was going to get me. Now each night when I go to bed I pray before I go to sleep. Boy! I sure feel great about sleeping by myself.

5. **<u>Math</u>** - I thought it was too hard but with lots of help from my teachers, family, me asking lots of questions and practicing on my own It's not that hard after all.

6. **<u>Leaving all my friends and family</u>** - was a little hard but I'm okay. My parents said I would make new friends. You know; they were right. There are a few kids in my neighborhood that I'm proud to call some really great companions who I look forward to us becoming really great friends someday.

7. **<u>Moving to a new city</u>** - was so scary to me but I'm okay now.

8. **<u>The first day of school</u>** - I was SOOO scared because I hardly knew anyone. We had only been in our new hometown a few months and now my school was new! The school building was so huge and gigantic, everybody was so much taller than me. I told my mom that they look like giants! It seems like, since I'd been there a for a while, I think time kind a helped me overcome that fear.

9. **<u>Meeting new people</u>** - I have a fear that other people won't like or except me. But my parents always tell me & my siblings never be afraid of someone not liking us or accepting us. Just be confident in who we are and how God made us. Never try to make others accept us. Just be yourself; especially at school because you are not there just to make friends you are there to learn and get a good education in order for you to be successful in life.

I'm glad that I faced and have now overcome my fears! If they happen to come back, I sure am glad I better understand and now know little bit about how to handle them.

BELIEVE IN YOURSELF

To sum it all up, you and I don't have to be afraid of anything or anyone. We don't have to prove to anyone that we are good at something or that we are better than them. It's no need for that. All we have to do is be confident, have courage, and believe in ourselves. My motto from here on out is Just do it! Don't Let Fear Stop you! We've got this my friends! We can do this! We can positively do and be anything we want to be! We are not afraid, we are courageous winners!

IT'S TIME TO PLAY THE GAME!

Now that I know I don't have to be afraid, scared, fearful or try to prove myself; I just have one more thing I need to overcome right now. I kind a talked and day dreamed about in the beginning of this book but I didn't get the chance to put this on my list of fears to face and overcome; and that is to play a real game of soccer. However, with all my courage and confidence, I'm now ready to join a real team. I think it's time to play the game and WIN!

Hey! before I end this story, I was thinking when I grow up I'm going to run for President! Nothing can stop me now! Can you hear the crowd cheering? Oh, wait, there I go dreaming again. I really want to be an Olympic gold medalist, greatest of all time, female soccer player when I grow up!

Listen my friends, always be confident & brave and never LET FEAR STOP YOU!

THE END!

A THOUGHT FROM MICAIAH

Hey, before you close my book I want to tell you something, I just had a thought, If someone is bullying you or you know of someone who at this moment is being bullied or maybe the person is a bully themselves; take a stand and say something. Did you know that if you don't say anything to someone about it, that this could be fear stopping you? The best thing to do is tell an adult. This can be someone that you trust such as your parents or maybe a teacher. Bullying must be stopped immediately!

If this is happening or has happened and you get the courage to say something about it, Listen, that doesn't mean that you are a tattler. You may be saving a life or keeping you or someone from a dangerous situation. Bullying is serious. When it comes to bullying, you must stand up and don't be afraid to tell. And always remember, don't let fear stop you.

Hey! Cyber bullying is not okay either!!

ABOUT THE AUTHOR

Micaiah Crenshaw is a very creative, intelligent, innovative and caring 9-year-old that has a passion and drive to be successful. She is always willing to help others. She's currently in the 4th grade and is very excited about learning, She adores her teacher Mrs. Gonzalez and is proud of her school.

This is Micaiah's first children's book! She along with her family and friends are amazed and very proud of her efforts and accomplishments!

Hey guys I just wanted to give you a little heads up on my new book that's coming out! Yay! It's about bullying. that's all I can tell you right now because I don't want to spoil it! Well see you guys later!

STAY CONNECTED WITH MICAIAH BY FOLLOWING HER ON:

www.instagram.com/@micaiahjada

www.facebook.com/micaiahcrenshaw

*For God hath
not given us the spirit of fear; but of power,
and of love, and of a sound mind.*

2 Timothy 1:7 (KJV

NOTES

Illustrations by: Danelayers & inspired Corliss Meredith (Mom)

Book cover created by nirjhar625 & inspired by: Corliss Meredith Mom)

Scripture quotations marked KJV: Are from the Holy Bible, King James Version